Hartington
and Longnor

Guide & Souvenir

Lindsey Porter

A E

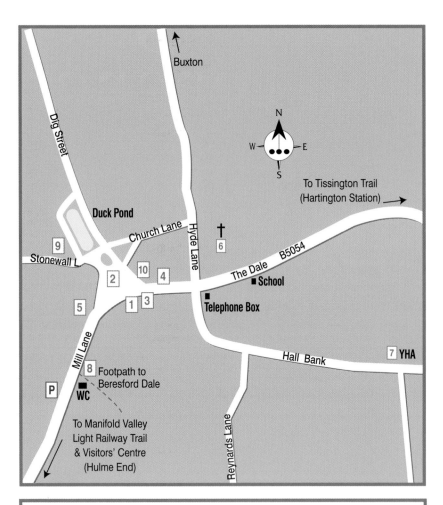

Hartington

1	Post Office / Café	7	Hartington Hall YHA	8	Rooke's Pottery
2	Bus Stop	4	Villages Stores	9	Rooke's Pottery
3	Devonshire Arms P.H.	5	Charles Cotton Hotel	10	Hart in the Country
		6	St Giles Church		

Hartington

Hartington is situated where Hartington Dale reaches the broad river meadows of the River Dove. It is on the B5054 between Warslow and Newhaven and a couple of miles off the A515 Buxton to Ashbourne road.

It is probable that there was originally a stream (the River Harden) flowing across what is now the Market Place, but it now flows through a culvert beneath the road surface. The stream may be seen flowing through 'The Stanner' (an opening on the culvert) at the head of Stonewall Lane and close to the village mere or duck-pond. The mere possibly dates from the seventeenth century but not earlier.

Top left: St Giles church **Top right:** Winter in Hartington
Above: A view from the village pond

The Devonshire Arms

The oldest buildings (except for the church) date from the early years of the seventeenth century. Hartington Hall, dating from 1611, is probably the earliest complete surviving house although a previous building existed upon the site. Many properties in the district were rebuilt in stone during the seventeenth and eighteenth centuries.

A good proportion of the older buildings have date-stones. Together with the variety of styles of vernacular architecture it makes a wander around the village worthwhile. Look out particularly for the arcaded front of the village shop, at one time both a shop and The Volunteer Inn and later, the Co-op. It was originally built in 1836 as a shop and has an unusual carving on its façade. It displays a man holding a set of scales and flanked by two women. To the right of the shop is a row of low terraced houses with the date-stone '1777 T & JC'. They were built by Thomas and Jane Cantrell as cotton workers cottages. Their cotton mill was directly opposite on the site of Minton House. Several houses were faced with cut limestone blocks with gritstone used for door and window surrounds. The Charles Cotton Hotel is interesting in this respect as a comparison may be made with the style of the extension, which has the date-stone 1864 tucked under the ridge on the gable end.

Charles Cotton (1630-1687)

Hartington's hotel, The Charles Cotton, formerly known as The Sleigh Arms (pronounced 'slee'), was named after a local family. It was possibly changed to The Charles Cotton c.100 years ago.

Cotton lived at Beresford Hall, to the west of Beresford Dale, south-west of Hartington and adjacent to the River Dove. He inherited the hall from his father in 1658. He clearly had talent as a writer and contributed to the 5th edition of Izaak Walton's book, *The Compleat Angler*. This was originally published in 1653 and at more than 300 new printings is one of the most reprinted books. It is still available and in print today.

The hall was demolished in the late 1850s with the intention of it being rebuilt, but this did not happen. Today two buildings survive on the former estate, a tower and the most interesting is Cotton's fishing house (or temple) of 1674 (not open), built on a bend of the river in Beresford Dale. Today it is on private land but obscured from the footpath by trees and shrubs.

Above: The Old School House, Church Lane **Top right:** Cottages, Market Place **Above right:** Fountain, Market Place **Below:** The Old Cheese Shop

Well dressings & Wakes Week

Hartington Well Dressings coincide with Wakes Week and are held on the second Saturday in September. Various other events take place on the day.

Clearly some of the houses were built to reflect the status of the occupier. For example Hartington Hall was occupied by the Bateman family until 1934. It was then let to the Youth Hostel Association, who finally purchased the hall and farm in 1948 for £6,000.00.

Adjacent to The Old Vicarage and the mere is Springfield House, a well proportioned house, now the focus of many photographs. This was built in 1790, on earlier 16th century foundations and is very similar to Watergap Farm in Dig Street. The latter is dated 1766 at the front and 1693 on the smaller building at the rear. Beyond Watergap Farmhouse is Pool Hall and Moat Farm.

Above: St Giles church and (below) Hartington Flower Festival held in June.

The latter includes traces of a medieval house which formerly existed within a moat on this site. Church Street has a couple of old schools, one dated 1758 (see map of village) as well as The Old Vicarage at the Market Place end of the street dated 1789. This building was originally built by the Duke of Devonshire for the manager of Ecton Copper Mine, Cornelius Flint. The Dukes owned much of the village and the oldest son of each Duke carries the title of the Marquis of Hartington.

Many houses in the village are of no special appeal individually. Collectively, however, they create street scenes of great charm and character, helping to contribute to the reputation of this justly popular village. Situated on the hillside above the village sits St. Giles' Church. It dates from the late thirteenth century and contains remnants of early wall paintings. The village was well established when the church was built. It was mentioned in the Domesday Book and the market rights were granted by King John in 1203 – the first in the Peak District. Although it has been many years since a market was held in the square, Hartington still has an air of prosperity.

Hartington Hall

Hartington Hall, situated near the top of Hall Bank was originally built in 1350 as a priory of the nuns of St. Clare. The church had been conferred upon the order in 1291, so presumably it had been completed by this date. Bonnie Prince Charles is alleged to have slept here on his retreat from Derby, although in reality one wonders whether he or one of his generals was actually quartered here. The small panelled room where he is supposed to have slept still survives. The present house was built in 1611 in the popular local style with projecting side wings. The sides and rear were added in 1861.

The farm buildings were also added in 1859. Bay windows to the ground and first floor were added on the west side in 1911, 300 years after the front was built. Today the hall is the oldest surviving youth hostel in the Peak District and one of the most popular. It has a bar that stocks local ales, one of which is brewed near the village and a restaurant serving locally sourced produce. Both are open to the public.

Many of the field's stone walls near to the village date from early times and they are shown on an old estate map of 1617. Further away, the old strip fields are still visible by the undulating strips of land. These were created by the farmer ploughing his strip by turning the soil over into the middle of the strip from each side.

The field boundaries over these strips were the result of the inclosures of c.1808. Many of the farm extensions (including new construction of houses and outbuildings on the former Devonshire estate) date from the years following the inclosures. The slates on the roof of these buildings came from North Wales, being delivered to Leek or Cheddleton wharves on the Caldon Canal. They are likely to have come from Bethesda Quarry and been shipped via Runcorn.

Today the village serves not only as a stopping place for day visitors but also for longer stays using local accommodation – including the refurbished Charles Cotton Hotel, youth hostel and several B & Bs.

Upper Dove Valley

Pilsbury Castle

Upper Dove Valley near Hartington

A CIRCULAR FAMILY WALK FROM HARTINGTON
(3 MILES)

From the centre of the village proceed to Hall Bank with quite a steep short climb up a minor road. The rest of the route is on undulating shale tracks.The track between A and B on the map could be difficult for pushchairs.

Two other routes are suggested as you can see from the map. It is always advisable to wear stout shoes or boots and have a warm jacket when walking in the Peak District.

1. From the centre of the village walk back along the B5054 to pass the Beresford Tea Rooms and the Post Office. Just before the telephone kiosk and by the brown YHA sign on the left, turn right up Hall Bank.

2. In about ½ mile and having passed the youth hostel turn right signed "Biggin" onto the cycle route 54.

3. Follow this shale walled track for ¾ mile [20 minutes]. Ignore paths off and just after a track on the left turn right.

4. Follow this walled, shale, stone and grass track for just under ½ mile. At a junction of tracks turn right to walk to a metalled lane.

5. Ignore the Wolfscote Grange route to keep straight on along the minor road [Reynards Lane].

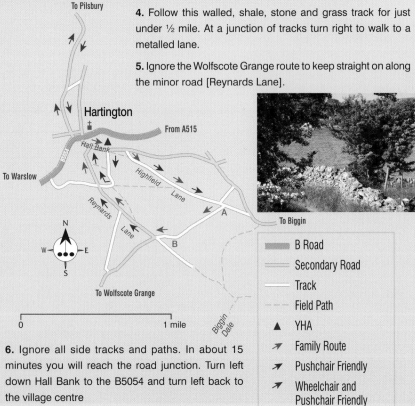

To Pilsbury

Hartington

From A515

Hall Bank

To Warslow

Highfield Lane

Reynards Lane

A

B

To Biggin

N
W E
S

To Wolfscote Grange

0   1 mile

Biggin Dale

▰▰▰	B Road
═══	Secondary Road
───	Track
- - -	Field Path
▲	YHA
⬈	Family Route
⬈	Pushchair Friendly
⬈	Wheelchair and Pushchair Friendly

6. Ignore all side tracks and paths. In about 15 minutes you will reach the road junction. Turn left down Hall Bank to the B5054 and turn left back to the village centre

Walk by Pat Tidsall

Longnor

This small moorland community sits on the side of a ridge between the valleys of the Dove and Manifold. Although a community existed here as long ago as the 13th century (the church was originally founded in 1223) and it had an ancient market, it grew as a crossing point of various packhorse and later turnpike roads.

Longnor

The packhorse road from Cheshire, or at least perhaps the main one, crossed the River Dane heading for Flash village (the highest in England). It then took the lane, now tarmac covered, from The Travellers Rest Inn along Edge Top between the Dove and Manifold valleys heading for Hollinsclough and then onto Longnor.

Longnor developed in the 18th century. The corn-mill (on the road to Leek) was rebuilt in 1769, but like Crowdecote mill on the River Dove was probably much older. Many of the village centre properties date from this era, with the establishment of inns and accommodation for travellers, drovers etc.

The number of tradesmen in the village was substantial for the area and reflected the trade generated by the numerous travellers and traders passing through.

There appears to have been a depot here where carriers could deliver parcels and cargoes for collection by other carriers for onward movement to another destination. Other arrangements existed whereby goods were also left at a particular pub for collection. The copper mine at Ecton, down the river, regularly did this.

An idea of the amount of packhorse traffic which used to pass between Longnor and Leek can be seen to the south-west of the village at Lane Farm.

Here is a huge holloway, where a cutting has been created by erosion from the feet of horses. It is some 20ft (6.5m) deep and can be visited as the packhorse way is still a public footpath. It is the deepest holloway in the area and probably in the Peak District.

Despite all the through traffic, the community was either self-sufficient or relied on locally produced materials when it could. Locally grown oats were ground at

Top: Market Hall

Above: Market Hall, toll charges

Longnor and Crowdecote mills to produce oatmeal. Stone and bricks came from local sources for building. The stone was actually mined at Daisy Knoll mine on the road to Hollinsclough and bricks were made at Reapsmoor 3 miles (5km) to the south. Several buildings in the village are built with stone from Daisy Knoll. The former Crewe and Harpur Arms Hotel, (now private appartments) in the village was made from bricks made there and it probably sold large quantities to Ecton Mine, the first mine in the country to pass 1,000ft (308m) deep.

Coal for the village was mined on Axe Edge and Goldsitch Moss a few miles to the west. Lime came from Buxton to the north and several local farms had their own kiln to burn limestone and reduce it to lime for spreading on the fields to neutralise acidic soils and also for mortar.

By the early 19th century the village had seven public houses (today there are only two).

However, Longnor's development stalled in the 19th century. Despite talk of extending the Manifold Light Railway to the village, this remained just an idea. The village was bypassed by the Ashbourne-Buxton line in 1890 and other communities – Leek, Buxton, Bakewell and Ashbourne all grew at Longnor's expense.

Today this small village is a good centre for exploring the upper Dove and Manifold Valley, or stopping off for a while. Many of the packhorse roads are now footpaths threading through quiet, attractive and relatively unknown countryside. Paths down both river valleys can be used with paths crossing both of them to make a good circular route. There are several such paths, so you can pick out a route that suits the distance you wish to walk. With a 1:50000 Explorer O.S. Map you can follow the paths easily as they show every field you pass through. Most of the paths are sufficiently well-used to be easily identified on the ground.

Longnor Today

The village centre has changed little since Georgian times, with the notable exception of the Market Hall, which was replaced by the current structure in 1873. It still has the toll charges exhibited on the front of the building dating from 1904. It is now a craft centre, displaying local artists work, all manner of different crafts and locally made Fox Country Furniture. It does also have a good tearoom offering light lunches and homemade cakes and scones.

The Horseshoe Inn apparently dates from 1609, in which case it has probably been re-fronted. More recently its façade was used as the outside of the 'Black Swan' in ITV's Peak Practice. The nearby Cheshire Cheese Inn, also records the trading links of the past with cheeses from Cheshire. These were presumably traded from a cheese store opposite the inn possibly dating as far back as 1464. This was demolished as it jutted out into the road. The 19th century cheese factory at Reapsmoor to the south produced Derby cheese and there was another cheese factory at Glutton Bridge on the River Dove to the north.

The village car-park is on the Market Place along with the village shop and newsagents. There are also public toilets here.

The church's first record is of its construction in 1223. Replaced in Elizabethan times, it was rebuilt in 1781 and this is the building that survives today. Altered to increase the height some thirty years later, further alterations were made following a fire in 1883. In the churchyard is the grave of William Billinge born in a cornfield at Fairfieldhead. He died in 1791 at the age of 112 following a prolonged military career recorded on his gravestone.

Above: Well Dressing **Above right:** The church St Bartholomew

On Leek Road is Longnor mill, slowly being restored. There is a record of it in 1404 and this was rebuilt in 1605 followed by a subsequent rebuild in 1769 (excessive vibration often being the cause, when the structure was insufficient to withstand it). The small 14ft (4m) waterwheel would seem to point to the mill being limited in its power, possibly by there being insufficient water power to drive a larger wheel.

The nearby mills at Crowdecote and Hartington, in Hartington Manor, ground oats occasionally barley and made malt for beer making. It is likely that other local parishes such as Longnor did the same.

Trails and Cycle Routes

Trails and cycle routes in the White Peak offer magnificent views across the dales, hills, farmland and villages. Flowers on hillsides and in hay meadows are plentiful and colourful in spring and summer. Autumn and winter are equally beautiful with leaves changing colour and frost glistening on cold winter days. Cycles can be hired and free leaflets are available from tourist information centres.

Tissington Trail

Opening in 1899, the Tissington Trail was one of the last Victorian railway lines. Another was the Manifold Valley Light Railway.

Limestone was sent to industrial areas from local quarries and also milk was supplied to London. In 1967 the railway closed and the trail was created.

Hartington Station signal box beside the trail is preserved and serves as an Information Centre. It is open on Saturday, Sunday and Bank Holidays and provides refreshments, parking and toilets.

The Tissington Trail has a firm crushed limestone surface making it ideal for all users. However, if you are cycling from Ashbourne, bear in mind that the trail rises uphill continually to Biggin and is fairly flat to the end of the trail at Hurdlow, on the Longnor-Monyash road.

The southern end of the trail takes you into Ashbourne via an electrically lit 600m long tunnel. There is a car park, cycle hire, toilets and refreshments at Ashbourne. Tissington has toilets and refreshments on the trail and a tearoom in the village.

Manifold Valley Light Railway

Built in 1904, the Leek & Manifold Valley Light Railway used this track to transport dairy products from the valley to the main railway south at Waterhouses. It was narrow gauge, and built to a rail width of 30in. The coaches were Colonial in style and painted primrose yellow. They must have looked picturesque when seen in the valley.

The railway closed in 1934. One section of the track from Swainsley to just south of Wetton Mill became a new road, part of a walking and cycling route from Waterhouses to Hulme End. The old waiting room at Hulme End is preserved and now an Information Centre. It has a model layout of the station area with a small scale engine and rolling stock, worked electrically.

The flowers are plentiful in

spring and summer and it is a most enjoyable trail to wander or cycle along.

The trail has a good surface and is ideal for wheelchairs, pushchairs and cyclists. The section from Wetton Mill to Swainsley does, however, have motor traffic. This stretch also includes a 100m tunnel at Swainsley. It is illuminated but not really recommended for wheelchairs or pushchairs. It is suggested that you take the old road on the other side of the river which now sees little motor traffic from Wetton Mill to Swainsley.

There are toilets and a tearoom at Wetton Mill and a pub, The Manifold Inn, at Hulme End that also offers accommodation.

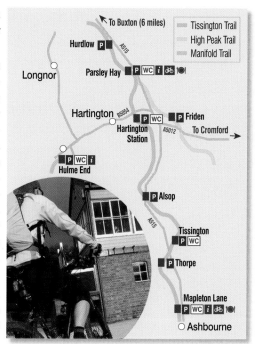

High Peak Trail

The Cromford & High Peak Railway was one of the first railways in the world. Built between 1825 and 1830, it linked the Peak Forest Canal to the Cromford Canal – a distance of 33 miles (53km). Even today the old stations are still referred to as wharfs.

Cycling on the Tissington Trail (image courtesy of © Visit Peak District & Derbyshire)

Accommodation

Lists of various types of accommodation may be obtained from Tourist Information Centres. There is a full range of serviced accommodation: hotels, guest houses, bed & breakfast, farm houses, youth hostels, camp and caravan sites.

Tourist Information Centres

Ashbourne	☎ 01335 343666
Leek	☎ 01538 483741
Buxton	☎ 01298 25106
Manifold Valley	☎ 01298 84679

Other Information

There is a public toilet in Hartington, adjacent to the pottery on Mill Lane. Longnor's public toilet is adjacent to The Market Hall (Longnor Craft Centre) on the Market Place.

Cycle Hire Centres

Ashbourne	☎ 01335 343156
Parsley Hay	☎ 01298 84493
Waterhouses	☎ 01538 308313
Brown End Farm	☎ 01538 308313 m: 07779 320975
Manifold Valley	☎ 01538 308609

Free Peak Cycle Hire leaflets available from all Tourist Information Centres
Email: cyclehire@peakdistrict.gov.uk

Published by **Ashbourne Editions**
The Oaks, Moor Farm Road West, Ashbourne ☎ (01335) 347349 Fax: (01335) 347303

1st edition: ISBN: 978-1-873-775-34-9

Printed by: Gutenburg Press Ltd, Malta
Design: Ceiba Graphics
Photography: © Mark Titterton / Ceiba Graphics (www.ceibagraphics.co.uk)
www.visitpeakdistrict.com: page 15 bottom
Acknowledgement: The author would like to thank Pat Tidsall for supplying a walk. Other circular walking books by Pat are available locally.

Front cover: view of Hartington **Back cover top** (l-r): A view of Longnor, Cottages in Longnor, Morris Men at Hartington Well Dressing/ Wakes Week **Back cover main:** Spring time in the Upper Dove Valley between Hartington and Longnor